T0210116

THE BIBLE,

"The perfect tool for the Devil"

NOW

THE DEVIL IS IN THE

WHITE HOUSE

LARRY D. HALL

authorHOUSE

AuthorHouse™
1663 Liberty Drive
Bloomington, IN 47403
www.authorhouse.com
Phone: 1 (800) 839-8640

Published by AuthorHouse 01/25/2020

ISBN: 978-1-7283-4487-4 (sc)
ISBN: 978-1-7283-4489-8 (hc)
ISBN: 978-1-7283-4488-1 (e)

Library of Congress Control Number: 2020901655

"Use this as God's rattling call"

To Whom it may concern:

This book was written by the request of God. He had me to write it to show that the Bible is being use by the Devil to persuade man to turn against God. The Bible is still the word of God 'but' the Devil have enter into it, causing man to use it for all his wrong durings. Now the time has come for man to decide (good over evil).

God has spoken, "believe it or not at the cost of loosing your soul".

It was written by God and me, I wrote it to educate black people, and made white people see the error of their ways.

"JESUS CHRIST or the ANTICHRIST... WHOSE SIDE ARE YOU ON"?

WE ARE NEARING THE MIDNIGHT HOUR...We don't know the DAY or the HOUR, but it is clearly IMMINENT!

"Choose you this day whom ye shall serve..."

God/Larry D. Hall

Contents

Introduction

THIS IS THE REASON God chose me to write this (he saved me for it).

When I was growing up, I had a saying, "live fast die young have a good looking corpus". I did everything in my power throughout the years to make that a true statement. I now know why I failed. God had his arms around me then.

Three times God showed me death, the first time when I was young, the second time in Vietnam, but the third time he made me know it was him who saved me. I was trapped in the door of my car with it in gear and moving (I couldn't stop it), someone came from (I don't know from where) he stop the car, and was gone. I can't explain it, but this is what happen. God sent an angel to save me.

Then, he showed me in a vision (that he saved me the 2 other times). The first time, when I was young some people tried to kill me (3) times with a razor and gun (shooting at me 6 times missing all 6), God saved me by making the (6) shot miss, and not allowing them to have seven. The second time in Vietnam a VC terrorist tried to kill me (3) times the third time God controlled my shots (I shot at him 6 times all hitting him) killing him. God made their shots miss and my shots hit.

Twice the Devil tried to take me (the number 6, the number of shots 6, 6), God said, "no" but the third time he tried to take me "God" sent his angel to save, and protect me. This meant (6) evil, against (3) Trinity (God wins), and sent an angel.

Throughout my life, I have been comp-ailed to do the right thing, although I did a lot of wrong things (how can that be?) the Devil was trying to take my soul, but God won.

So, my message from "God" to man 'is' "get your life in order, then everything else will be in order, then you will be playing a winning hand".

Remember God is 'everything' he knows everything, so you can't lie to him only to yourself. He knows your inter-most thoughts 'so' be very careful of what you think.

In starting, something need to be said, "the state of America today" the Devil is in the White House, and we are at a cross rode (time to decide). If God knows everything, why didn't he stop it? Because the devil always end up where he belongs in HELL (the White House) today, Now it's time for American's to decide what house they want to live in (God's house) or (the Devil's house).

When you reap what you soy (see the error of your ways) that's what "Heaven" or "HELL" is like.

The meek shall inherit the "earth", so says God.

Power and Greed is the combination to the lock (that unlock) the door to "HELL", so says the Devil.

So, all Americans that decided with evil (the White House now), will be judged by their actions (be very careful of your actions). The Devil have now drawn sides (evil against good) it's now time to pick a side (the survivable of all man-kind is at stake). American's can no longer sit on the side line (it's time to get in the game) the game for good verses evil "winner take all".

"JESUS CHRIST or the ANTICHRIST... WHOSE SIDE ARE YOU ON"?

WE ARE NEARING THE MIDNIGHT HOUR... We don't know the DAY or the HOUR, but it is clearly IMMINENT!

God said, "Choose you this day whom ye shall serve..."

I.

FIRST OFF, HOW CAN anything past down from generations to generations be believed anyway. Man only sees what he wants to see, it has nothing to do with the truth. So, how can people put their fate in something that was control for thousands of years by man (white man) the Bible. The white man have never given the black man anything that was good for him 'so' why would the Bible be any different?

Just like the constitution was written by (white men) for (white men), black people were consider 2/3 human, 'so' we didn't count. Now that black people proved they are human, fought to be free (giving their lives), and getting the right to vote (please vote), the people that wrote the constitution is crying foul, now that it is starting to do what it was written to do (for them), it's now starting to do for everyone (they want to change it).

In the beginning God created heaven, earth, and all that is in it. After creating the world, God looked around and saw something was missing, so God created "man". After creating man (God is of all things), he knew man would be lonely (he needed a compantant), so God took a rib from Adams side and created "woman".

God had made man and woman Adam/Eve put them in paradise. All they had to do too remaind there is not eat fruit from the forbidden tree. God said, "you can eat from all the other trees in the garden but not from this tree" Adam ask, "why"? God said, "Because the fruit from this tree is forbidden fruit".

Because if they eat fruit from this tree (they would know evil) then they would have to leave the Garden of Eden because they would then know good and evil. But if they did not eat from the forbidden tree Adam and Eve could live in the Garden of Eden forever. God left the chose up to them.

The Devil or Satan was waiting in the garden (he was waiting for a chance to persuade Eve) to convince her to eat from the forbidden tree. So the Devil waited for Adam and Eve to be apart. Adam had fallen asleep.

Then the Devil saw his chance. Satan called out to Eve, "Eve come here taste this juice apple" Eve said, "God said not to eat fruit from this tree" Satan said, "if you eat fruit form this tree you be as wise as him that's why" So, Eve was persuade by the Devil to eat from the forbidden tree. THEN Eve convince Adam to eat from the tree. They had disobey God buy eating the fruit.

When God came to the garden looking for Adam/Eve they were hiding. Then God called out to them. "Adam/Eve why are you hiding"? Eve answered, "Because he are naked" God ask, "How do you know you are naked"? Adam answered, "Because he eat from the forbidden tree" God said, "you will now have to leave the Garden of Eden.

Now Adam/Eve would have to go out in the world and survive by the sweat of their labor. Now they would have children and suffer the pain of child birth.

An angel came to Adam. He said Jesus would sacrifice his life for us someday. It would be his gift to us. The sacrifices helped Adam and Eve think about the sacrifice of Jesus.

God had made man and woman (put them in paradise) all man had to do too remain in paradise is not eat from the forbidding tree (the fruit). Since God knows everything, he knew man would eat the fruit from the forbidding tree. But still he gave man a chance to serve him, knowing he could be persuade by the Devil to eat the fruit.

God knew man would be unable to resist gifts, this is the weakness of man. Man would risk losing his place in paradise for the sake of gold when he was already richer that he would ever be. The greed of man will always be one of the Devil's best tools. All the Devil have to do is show man a shinning object (he will sell his soul), to the Devil.

For Adam/Eve disobeying God, they were cast out of the the garden of paradise. Now God would show them what life is like when you disobey him. Because of their disobeyness all the human race would now suffer for the sins of one man "Adam".

God gave them 2 sons Cain/Abel and (the Devil) cause a rift between them. Since they had disobeyed God (he didn't protect them from the Devil) since listing to the Devil was the reason they were cast out of paradise in the first place.

This is where God allow the Devil to work on Cain (influeing his mind) causing Cain to kill Abel and then being casted out into the darkness.

Adam and Eve would have other children not of God's blessings. They were born without the word of God, they had no rules to guide them (such as the Bible). This was the beginning of sin. Man had no way of knowing right from wrong.

Adam had been persuaded by Eve, who listing to the Devil to take a bite from fruit of the forbidding tree.

Causing them to be casted out into an unholy world. Their children to produce unholy offsprings. Making the world an unholy place.

During this time a mighty king was ruling an unholy kingdom. The Devil had empower him with all kinds of richness. He grew so powerful, he thought he was a God (not the God) until the Devil persuade him to challenge God.

This king name "Uzziah's" that though he was a God, built a very, very tall stairway to the sky. He climb to the top and challenge God (the God) the all powerful God. God answer his challenge by turning his kingdom into a nightmare.

God cause his people to speak in different languages, no one understood what the other one was saying, and the king couldn't understand what anybody was saying. Because of him challenging God his kingdom was now a sea of confusion. The Devil had showed another one of his greatest weapons (the power to persuade).

The Devil use this weapon to make a man think he was a God. Then force him to challenge God 'if' you challenge God you will lose. He lose all the richness of his kingdom because of this.

His people were then spread out in all directions north, south, east, and west. People that spoke the same languages went in the same directions, causing divisions in the world.

A world that was unholy. The word of God was not being taught.

Evil begin to spread throughout the world, man was during unspeakable acts. This became so bad until God sent an angel to see if he could find one holy person in the city. He sent them to a city that was filled with all sorts of evil.

God said, "If the angel found one person that was holy in the city it would be spared". In a whole city of people you would think one person could be found, however there was a family that was holy. God said, "other than this family one other person that was holy, I would spare the city". No other person could be found.

So, God instructed the angel to allow them to leave the city and don't look back. Once safe out of the city, God order his angel to destroy the city. The noise from the city being destroyed cause someone to look back, God had instructed them not to look back. Because this person disobey God she was turned into stone.

Since woman had cause man to disobey God, now woman had disobey God, he then elevated man over woman to be the head of the house. God could no longer trust woman to not be persuade by the Devil 'or' obey him.

Once all the different races of people and different spoken languages were spread throughout the world. The

Devil had to find a race he could live within 'so' he looked over all the races and found the white race.

They process all the things the Devil needed (racist, greed, argant). Before all white people get angry, I'm not calling all of you Devils (just the greater number of you). The Devil felt he could persuade the rest of you.

The angels from the gaints that died in the flood were angels of the devil. When they returned to heaven, God kick them out, they returned to earth as demons. They process the souls of the white race (not all of you as I said before) just the greater number.

This cause your offspring to be born with evil inside, their offsprings, and the generations to generations of offsprings to be borned evil. Look at how you treated all other races throughout history. Only an evil person 'or' the Devil could do that.

No other race have done more un-speackable evil to other races than the white race (the Devil's race). God said, "all people are children of God".

To find out if you are not one of the greater number, take this test. When you have reap what you soy (seen the error of your ways), are you still pure in heart? Black people the same thing apply to you 'if' you're not living a Godly life.

Black people the Devil was the "Ark-Angel" the musician, 'so' stop during his work in your music. Stop using the Devil's lyrics to degrade your black sisters, and the killings of your black brothers. "You too will be judged" so says God.

Now all these black artists/actors such as (Kelly, Crosby) that has been so very, very, very blessed by God 'but' doing the bidding for the Devil, 'if' you think you're suffering on earth now wait until your soul's have to pay. "You too will be judged" so says God.

All the other ones that have been truly blessed by God, even if you don't think so. You may say, "God had nothing to do with your success" but, God allowed it to happen. So, you owe your success to God, now you have a duty to his people (black people) your people too help them advance, 'so' they too may become successful. Because all the success you think you have, God can take it away in the blink of an eye. "I'm the one that giveth or take it away", so says God.

Another thing, black people when your sons are killed during wrong, stop being so quick to blame the police even though they wrong us. God hold you responsible for your children, start teaching them the ways of God, he will then save them from the ways of man. I know, I was your son (God saved me) just like he will save your son. God said, "Bring the children unto me". "You too will be judged" so says God.

Also, all you so called neighborhood leader that only show up when something bad happens, where are you before it happen? You only want face time on TV. Same thing goes for the so called black preacher that preaches to the same people over and over (they supposed to be saved) what about the sinners that's in the streets that are not saved? So, if you want to do God's work go where his work needs to be done (where the sinners are). "You too will be judged", so says God.

Young black girls stop having babies because you think it's the thing to do. You're creating a life, a responsibility, and someone who will pattern their life after you. The combination to the keys to success is education 'or' talent not having babies. If you don't have talent get an education then you can give your children the keys to success.

Black people when will you stop letting white people use you as a prop. When white people use a so called black woman as a prop for black people during the Cohen hearings 'give me a break'. She stood there like a dummy, with no other reason for being there than a show. Then said later, "Trump wasn't a racists". If you need a so called black woman to say that (then you are a racists).

When you need someone to defend you being a racists (chances are) you are a racists. The lady in the House that questioned this racist's act, didn't call the person a racists, but he called himself that.

So, black people stop apologizing for telling the truth. The truth is the knife that cut the deepest, that's why it hurt the most. When you have seen the error of your ways, then faced the truth, it will then set you free.

I don't hold white people accountable for my future, 'so' I can't blame them for its outcome. If you thank that's what this book is about, then you're wrong. It was written to show black people who white people really are, in case black people have forgotten, 'to' show white people the error of their ways, how to be forgiven by Jesus, and saved by God.

Black people need to stop blaming white people for the outcome of their future and take control of it themselves. I once heard this older black man say, "This is the white man's world I'm just living in it", 'if' that's the way you think, then you're right. Because your world is what your mind say's it is. So, if you want the white man to control your world, keep thinking like that. But, if you want your world to change then change your mind (you will change your world).

Because I heard another older black man say, "we go where our mind's take us", 'so' let our mind's take us there.

To the minds of black people long ago. Now, let's be like the black race was long ago when they were the builders of moderate cizitization as we know it today. The black race was the most intelligent race of ancient times. These were the times of the greatest designs ever built (the pyramids).

No other design in the history of man have ever been built so perfect, as though it was built by the hands of God.

The black race is God's chosen people, although all people are children of God. Just like Jesus chose his disciples, God chose his people. That's the reason Jesus is black (he chose for God) who his people are, and who will be saved (through him).

To show you black people are God's people (he protects us from him) the sun. God put protections in black people's skin to protect them from the sun (it makes us stronger) the sun makes white people's skin burn causing death.

The sunshines (the light of God) on everything causing it to come to life, grass began to grow, trees start turning green, and flowers begin to bloom 'but' it will kill white people without skin protections (something that was given to black people by God) not brought from K-mart like white people do.

Now here's this so called black person with the last name 'West' that think he speaks for black people (what a joke), 'but' sold his soul to the Devil (Donald Trump). After the Devil is finished with him the Devil will abandon him same as he will Donald Trump. God don't save the Devil's rejects. Unless they repent all their sins, make atonement, ask Jesus forgiveness, and God can save them. God said, "We know not what day or hour" time is running out. "CHOOSE ye this day", so says God.

This will make white people even more confuse 'or' angry (Adam was black) the first man on earth. I don't have to tell white people what that means. God made Adam from the earth (all decendences of plantation owners) know the darker the soil the better the earth. However sand is white (God didn't make Adam from sand) he was made from the earth. Sand holds nothing not even water (nothing can be built on sand) 'but' the earth holds everything.

Adam was made from the earth of a garden (garden soil) the richest of all soils, and the darkest of all soils. The earth is made of soil (so was Adam). I rest my case.

To go a step more to show you black people are God's chosen people, every person he chose from the beginning to now was black (starting with Adam ending with Barack Obama). All the chosen one's in between was the decendences of Adam (who was black) case closed.

One more thing, God never chose a white man to serve him. The reason being, Satan and his demons process your race, 'so' you have to choose God to let him know you are not one of them (demons). God said, "Choose ye this day".

After black people die then get embalmed their bodies can remand out for a great period of time, not so for white people. God said, "From the earth we came to the earth we will return" BLACK.

Another thing, God charge the whole white race with sins to his people, until the white race repent for all their sins, make atonement, and ask Jesus forgiveness; God never will ask, "a white person to serve him", repent "whom shall you serve", so says God.

The Devil chose first (he was here before Christ) to decide what race he would process. The white race fit all his needs (dark souls). Jesus chose black people for God because their souls are pure. God said, "From the darkness into the light". The Devil thought white was the light 'but' God said "I am the light". I guess that's the reason white people think they're first in everything (the Devil chose them first) 'so' that will make you first (first in evil).

Now, black people go back and study your history, back to the time when black man was kings and rulers of great nations. You are the product of greatness 'so' never forget that.

During that time the world began to become so evil, until God decided something had to be done. Man no longer believed in God, he had started praying to things other than God. This cause God to become angry with his creation (man). You do not want to make God angry.

Man became so evil making the world a bad place to live that God decided, he had enough. He would now destroy his creation and start a new creation with a savor in mind. "Jesus Christ".

So, God told Noah, "build an ark larger enough for your family and all other creatures of the earth" he gave Noah the ark measurements. Noah and his family built the ark according to God's measurements.

When people saw Noah building a ship on dry land, they laugh, and though he was crazy. His family felt the same way, God hadn't spoken to them, they had to trust their father. Something young people need to do today (trust the father). When the father is during what God intended being the head of the household then the family should listen to the father.

God had promised Noah, "Once the ark is build, all creatures aboard, he would make it rain for 40 days and 40 nights" until the earth is completely cover with water. All living things that's not on board will be killed. God was now washing the earth of all its sins.

Once the art was built Noah and his family also went into the ark. Then God shut the door. Inside, Noah and his family waited. Just imagine you are there in the ark with them, waiting. Would there really be a flood as God said

Once safely inside the art, Noah and his whole family, God then directed the art to a location unknown to them. To a place where no other forms of life existed, now they would have to start God's new world. In a new land without sin, now God's word could be taught to the coming generations.

Everyone was laughing at Noah and during all kinds of evil things. They still did not believe that the Flood would come. They must have laughed more than ever. But they soon stopped laughing.

Then the rain begin to pour. It poured down from the sky as when you pour water from a bucket. Noah had been right! 'But' now it was too late (now for anybody else to get into the ark). The door had been closed tight by Jehovah.

It rain and rain until the whole world was covered with water. The water became like big rivers. It pushed over trees and rolled around big stones, and made a lot of noise. The people were afraid. They climbed up to higher ground. Oh, how they wished they had listened to Noah and gotten into the ark when the door was still open for them! But now it was too late.

The more it rain the higher the water kept getting, higher, and higher. For 40 days and 40 nights the water poured out of the sky. It rose up the sides of the mountains, and soon even the tallest mountains were covered. So just as God had said, all the people and animals outside the ark died. But everyone inside was safe. Flood waters begin to cover everything outside the ark

Noah and his sons had done a good job building the ark. The water lifted it up, and it floated right on top of the water. Then one day, after the rain stopped falling, the sun began to shine. What a sight it was! There was just one big ocean everywhere. And the only thing that could be seen was the ark floating on top.

God had washed the earth of all its evil. The giants were gone now. No more would they be around to hurt people. All of them had died, along with their mothers and the rest of the bad people.

The giants were angels of Satan they were not really human people like us. They were angels that had come down to live as men on earth. So when the Flood came, they did not die with the rest of the people. They stopped using the human bodies they had made, and went back to heaven as angels. But they were no longer allowed to be part of the family of God's angels. So they became the angels of Satan. They then came back to earth to process evil souls. Dark souls (hollow souls), the souls of the white race.

After the water was all gone God now made a wind blow, and the waters of the flood began to go down. Five months later the ark came to rest on the top of a mountain. Many more days passed, and those inside the ark could look out and see the tops of the mountains. The waters kept on going down and down.

To see if the waters has gone down enough Noah let a black bird called a raven out of the ark. It would fly away for a while and then it would come back, because it could not find a good place to land. It kept doing this and each time it returned, it would rest on the ark.

The next time Noah sent a dove out of the ark. But the dove came back too because it did not find a place to stay. Noah sent it out a second time, and it brought back an olive leaf in its beak. So Noah knew that the waters had gone down. Noah sent out the dove a third time, finally it found a dry place to live, and it didn't return.

Now that all the waters had gone down, God told Noah, go out of the ark take your whole family and the animals with you. They had been inside the ark for more than a whole year. So we can just imagine how happy they all were to be outside again and to be alive!

Once everything was over only eight people survived the Flood, but in time they increased to number many thousands. Then, 352 years after the Flood, Abraham was born. We learn how God kept his promise by giving Abraham a son named Isaac. Then, of Isaac two sons, Jacob was chosen by God.

Jacob had a big family of 12 sons and some daughters. Jacob's 10 sons hated their younger brother Joseph and sold him into slavery in Egypt. Later, Joseph became an important ruler of Egypt.

When a bad famine came, Joseph tested his brothers to see whether they had a change of heart. Finally, Jacob's whole family, the Israelites, moved to Egypt. This happened 290 years after Abraham was born.

For the next 215 years the Israelites lived in Egypt. After Joseph died, they became slaves there. In time, Moses was born, and God used him to deliver the Israelites from Egypt.

God had given man a chance to serve him 'but' man prove to be a servant unto himself. This cause God to look elsewhere for his servants (angels).

II.  The savor of the world "Jesus Christ," (God's 3rd angel).

❧❧❧

JESUS DIE ON THE cross for the sins of man 'so' that man could live the life he wanted. God gave his only son "Jesus" so man could be free to live (thank of that) all man have to do is live a righteous life (that's it).

Jesus begged his father on the cross to save him from death (although he knew he was already saved) in heaven. See, no man wants to die (not even Jesus) because when you die you leave all your family, and friends behind. You know, you will never see them again 'but' if you believe in God (you will) see them again (in heaven).

Jesus was born as the lest of 'us' to become the greatest of 'us", he was born in a stable among cattle and sheep. Not a place you would think for the savor of the world.

Jesus was the 3rd angel known to man, the 1st was the angel of Mercy, the angel of Death, and now the angel that saves all mankind "Jesus Christ". These are the servants of God, although there are many more angels on earth serving God. These are the ones the Devil know about. The other angels only God knows their indentfly. There are also many Devils on earth serving Satan 'so' man be aware.

Now I'm going to say something that will 'piss off" all people that think they're saved. Man cannot serve God (get over the shock), because God's needs are beyond man's understanding therefore he sent angels to earth to serve him (I know, an angel saved me).

When people become so called saved, the first thing they do is start eating and getting fat. God said, "Your body is your temple" 'so' if you were truly saved (by God) you would honor that, and not starting eating getting fat to dis-honoring that (causing bad health). The Devil don't care how your health is as long as you serve him. So, maybe the words from the Bible that was used to save you wasn't the words of God (because he cares).

God said, "Man is a servant unto me" that means if God calls you to serve him then you serve God. Until then live a Godly life, you may be forgiven by Jesus, and God will save you.

Man only serve the needs of man not even the needs of others. Just look at the world today, all these people serving their own needs when they should be serving the needs of the people that sent them there. God is watching you when you use the Bible to in-vain his name. When you're following the Devil (Donald Trump) and using his name. You can't know God and follow the Devil. "Chose ye this day' 'you can't serve 2 masters", so says God.

However you can come to truly know God and be saved (after death). Death is eternal mind 'so' if your mind is a Godly mind (you live in heaven forever). Jesus said, "Only the pure in heart shall see God".

So, man can only serve God (by living a righteous life), because man only knows the needs of man (God knows the needs of everything). So, going to church "or' praying don't mean you have lived a righteous life (but God knows).

The second you except God has you savor (you are saved), he will make your mind (a righteous mind). God said, "I am the truth and the light".

Because God knows everything (he knew man could never truly serve him), the faults of man or to great (greed, selflessness, pride) would keep man from serving God. To be saved is to except God as your savor (period).

Since God don't save man through man, he save man by the power of God. When he saved you on earth, then you become one of his angels on earth (same as Jesus) to serve him (same as the angel of death). That don't mean you shouldn't be good (you will be judge later). When you have been saved on earth (you are saved in heaven) no need to be judged.

However God do save you through someone else 'if'' that someone else has been saved by God. People like (mother's, father's, preachers) that serve 'people' that God save (will be saved) in heaven.

Before Jesus was born there was an evil king name "Herod", he heard of the coming of a savor. So, the king had all young male babies under 2 years old killed 'but' God had sent an angel to warm them.

Mary and Joseph was able to take baby Jesus to a safe place. The 3 wise men had seen a star in the sky that lead them to the place where baby Jesus was laying in straw in a stable, among animals of the stable.

An angel had come to Joseph and told him his wife "Mary" was going to have a baby that wasn't his (think of that), what man alive today would except that. No way could you convince any man of that (that his wife hadn't cheaped on him). But Joseph was a man of God, he knew Mary was a woman of God 'so' he knew it was a birth from God (the son of God).

After Jesus was born and angels showed Mary and Joseph how to save him from the raft of king "Herod". He grew up as all other young boys did at that time.

After the death of King Herod, Mary and Joseph was able to return to the place they had left. They could now return to

Galilee, and live in the place they grew up, Nazareth. Now they could raise their son without fear.

Look at the young boy talking to these older men. They are teachers in God's temple at Jerusalem. And the boy is Jesus. He has grown up quite a bit. Now he is 12 years old.

The teachers are very surprised that Jesus knows so much about God and the things written in the Bible. But why aren't Joseph and Mary here too? Where are they? Let's find out.

Every year Joseph brings his family to Jerusalem for the special celebration called the Passover. It's a long trip from Nazareth to Jerusalem. No one has a car, and there are no trains. They didn't have them in those days. Most of the people walk, and it takes them about three days to get to Jerusalem.

By now Joseph has a big family. So there are some younger brothers and sisters of Jesus to look after. Well, this year Joseph and Mary have left with their children on the long trip back home to Nazareth

They think that Jesus is with others traveling along. But when they stop at the end of the day, they can't find Jesus. They look for him among their relatives and friends, but he's not with them! So they return to Jerusalem to look for him there.

At last they find Jesus here with the teachers. He is listening to them and asking questions. And all the people are amazed at how wise Jesus is. But Mary says: 'Child, why have you done this to us? Your father and I have been very worried trying to find you.'

'Why did you have to look for me?' Jesus answers. 'Didn't you know that I had to be in the house of my Father?'

Yes, Jesus loves to be where he can learn about God. Isn't that the way we should feel too? Back home in Nazareth, Jesus would go to meetings for worship every week. Because he always paid attention, he learned many things from the Bible. Let's be like Jesus and follow his example.

This is when the Devil got the idea of using the Bible to persuade man that it was God's words they were reading. So, the Devil enter into the words of the Bible as a means to persuade man.

God said, "do not use my name in vain", man has use the Bible to justify every wrong 'or' bad thing they have ever done. The thing that is use to in-vain his name will be rejected by "God". That don't mean that the Bible is not the word of God 'but' now only the Godly will know his words.

So, when you are reading the Bible be careful it's God's words you are reading. The Devils greatest weapon is the power of persuasion (what greater way to persuade man) than the Bible.

Remember the road to HELL is paved with good attentions. So, everything we thank is (good) may not be good in the eyes of God. The Devil have the power of persuasion to make man see something bad as good.

So, Jesus went throughout the land teaching the word of God, heeling the sick, making the blind see, and raising the dead. Preforming all kinds of great deeds in the name of God.

Still the people Jesus trusted the most, one of them betrayed him, another one denied knowing him, the rest was loyal to him.

The crucifixion of Jesus occurred in 1st-century Judea, most likely between AD 30 and 33. Jesus' crucifixion is described in the four canonical gospels, referred to in the New Testament epistles, attested to by other ancient sources, and is established as a historical event confirmed by non-Christian sources although there is no consensus among historians on the exact details.

According to the canonical gospels, Jesus was arrested and tried by the Sanhedrin, and then sentenced by Pontius Pilate to be scourged, and finally crucified by the Romans. Jesus was stripped of his clothing and offered wine mixed with myrrh or gall to drink after saying I am thirsty. He was then hung between two convicted thieves and, according to the Gospel of Mark, died some six hours later.

During this time, the soldiers affixed a sign to the top of the cross stating "Jesus of Nazareth, King of the Jews" which, according to the Gospel of John, was written in three languages.

They then divided his garments among themselves and cast lots for his seamless robe, according to the Gospel of John. According to the Gospel of John after Jesus' death, one soldier pierced his side with a spear to be certain that he had died, then blood and water gushed.

Jesus was betrayed by one of his followers to his enemies and sentence to die on the cross. He die on the cross for the sins of man. He saved 2 sinners on the cross before his own death, Jesus was able to save their sins (in heaven) but couldn't save his own life on earth.

He ask his father (God) to take this bitter cup from him. Still his father allowed his only son to die on the cross for the sins of man.

Now all man have to do is ask "Jesus" forgiveness and be saved by "God". God said, "I am the truth and the light no man cometh unto me unless threw the son" Jesus Christ.

III.

❧❦❧

THIS WAS ANOTHER MAN save on earth, that became an angel for God "Moses". He was saved from another king that ordered the killing of all young boys under 2 years old.

Moses was not a man of God in the beginning, he was raised by the Pharaohs, the enslaver of God's people. He grew up as a prince. See man will never know the person God save on earth to serve him. This is something that God keeps from the Devil, remember (the Devil) was here from the beginning also.

Moses was watching his sheeps when he saw something strange so he decided to go that a look. What Moses saw was a bush on fire but it did not burn up. So Moses thought, "I will go over and see this strange sight—why the bush on fire does not burn up."

Then God called out to Moses, God called to him from within the bush, "Moses! Moses!" And Moses said, "who are you, then God said "for the place where you are standing is holy ground, I am the God of your father, the God of Abraham, the God of Isaac and the God of Jacob." Moses could not look upon his face.

Then God said, "I have seen and heard the suffering of my people. I will send you to Pharaoh and tell him to let my people go. Moses ask, "What words shall I say to make Pharaoh listen". God said, "I will give you the right words to say". So now, go. I am sending you to Pharaoh to bring my people the Israelite s out of Egypt."

But Moses said to God, "Who am I that I should go to Pharaoh and bring the Israelite s out of Egypt?"

And God said, "I will be with you. And this will be the sign to you that it is I who have sent you: When you have brought the people out of Egypt, you will worship God on this mountain."

Moses said to God, "Suppose I go to the Israelite s and say to them, 'The God of your fathers has sent me to you,' and they ask me, 'What is his name?' Then what shall I tell them?"

God said to Moses, "I am who I am. This is what you are to say to the Israelites: 'I am has sent me to you.'" God also said to Moses, "Say to the Israelite s, 'The Lord, the God of your fathers—the God of Abraham, the God of Isaac and the God of Jacob—has sent me to you.' "This is my name forever, the name you shall call me from generation to generation.

Then God said, "go, assemble the elders of Israel and say to them, 'The Lord, the God of your fathers—the God of Abraham, Isaac and Jacob—appeared to me and said: I have watched over you and have seen what has been done to you in Egypt. And I have promised to bring you up out of your misery in Egypt into the land of the Canaanites, Hittites, Amorites, Perizzites, Hivites and Jebusites—a land flowing with milk and honey.'

Moses use the power of God to free his people from Pharaoh and take to a land of milk and honey. But each time there were problems the people question him, they still didn't truly believe in God, even after he spread the Red Sea so they could cross, and be saved from Pharaoh's army.

After crossing the Red Sea to safely, God told Moses, "to go up on the mountain, he will write his commandments in stone", the 10th commandments.

By the time Moses returned with God's commandments for man, (man had broken all of his commandments) they engaged in all kinds of sins. This angry God 'so' for their sins he denied them the lands of milk and honey.

God had showed Moses the lands, 'but' for their sins he would not allow Moses to take them. God made sure that all people that had disobey him was died before showing them the lands (he promised) the lands of milk and honey. See, when you disobey God it can cause your whole generation to suffer.

IV. *The Devil enslaves God's people*

❧❧❧

THE DEVIL (WHITE PEOPLE) kept God's people enslaved (black people) for over 400 years. Now say you're not the Devil. Only the Devil could do another race of people like that for so long. You didn't stop on your own (you where force to stop) then you fought, and still fighting to this today (too stop our rights as Americans). As I said before (white people) that take the test (if you're still pure in heart) you will be forgiven, through Jesus, and then be saved by God.

Because the Bible was use as the main weapon to keep black people enslaved for over 400 years. White preachers said, "This is the way God wanted it". All the white people in the churches during that time agreed with him. For over

400 years no white person stood-up to say it was evil 'so' that makes you all guilty of sins to God's people. God said, "Let my people go" 'but' you stilled kept them enslaved.

The year is 1780. In this year European traders will take thousands of Africans into slavery.

My name is Okechukwu. I am of the Igbo tribe. I don't know where I am. I don't know why I'm here. This isn't right.

I am Oyeladun of the Yoruba people. My story is like everyone's here-I had a good life and was taken. Other people here want to die-I am going to live.

I am Kwame. I was of the Asante people. I hope I will be Asante again but I'm not sure that is possible. I'll tell you what I've seen.

Okechukwu-Life before capture

My life was good before I was bought here. I miss it so much: the fields, the trees, the sunshine, my people-the Igbo.

Most of all I miss my mother and father. I dream about my mother. She is in a long blue dress she wove herself. She is cooking with the herbs and spices our neighbors have grown. Father is outside, chewing tobacco as he works at his fire.

Kwame-Life before capture

Like many others I was a goldsmith in our town, Kumasi, making jewelry and statues and other decorations. I learnt the skill from my father and he from his. We made many beautiful pieces-they made us wealthy. Our best customer was the Asantehene (although I did not agree with his taste!).

I don't know why the Asantehene lied. He said I cheated him; that I sold him poor quality gold. Other young men, some I know well, were accused of crimes as well. I think he planned to sell us to the white slave traders.

Some of the others tried to struggle against the guns and chains. There was no point. I saved my strength.

I didn't see my family. I fear for my wife, Kessie and our son, Adisa. I hope my father is there to care for them. I hope they are safe. I think the Asantehene will tell my father lies and try to cheat him again. I try to be angry, hoping it will stop me falling into misery like the others here but it is difficult.

"They sold us for money, and I myself was sold six times over, sometimes for money, sometimes for a gun, sometimes for cloth … It was about half a year from the time I was taken before I saw white people."

Nearly 250 years ago a 10-year-old African girl was kidnapped and transported to South Carolina, where she was renamed Priscilla and sold into slavery.

Unlike the ancestors of many African Americans who were brought to North America as slaves, Priscilla left a paper trail that tells her story and connects her to her living descendants.

"What makes Priscilla's Homecoming so special, and likely not to be repeated, is that Thomalind can trace her ancestry literally from the day the slave ship left Sierra Leone on April 9, 1756, to the present moment," said Joseph Opala, a historian at James Madison University in Harrisonburg, Virginia. "We're dealing with a 249-year paper trail."

Slavery was practiced throughout the American colonies in the 17th and 18th centuries, and African slaves helped build the new nation into an economic powerhouse through the production of lucrative crops such as tobacco and cotton.

For 400 years black people had to endure things that you couldn't dream of in your worst nightmare. The people that did it was white people (the Devil). Who other than the Devil could treat another human being this way? I know you said black people were, "2/3 human" 'but' that was a lie you told yourself.

Though the Emancipation Proclamation didn't officially end all slavery in America—that would happen with the passage of the 13th Amendment after the Civil War ended in 1865—some 186,000 black soldiers would join the Union Army, and about 38,000 lost their lives.

The 13th Amendment, adopted on December 18, 1865, officially abolished slavery, but freed blacks' status in the post-war South remained precarious, and significant challenges awaited during the Reconstruction period.

Former slaves received the rights of citizenship and the "equal protection" of the Constitution in the 14th Amendment and the right to vote in the 15th Amendment, but these provisions of Constitution were often ignored or violated, and it was difficult for former slaves to gain a foothold in the post-war economy thanks to restrictive black codes and regressive contractual arrangements such as sharecropping.

White people you much know for over 400 years you carried the sins of slaves. Jesus forgive those that are enslaved, and the sins belong to the salver. So, you have over 500 years of past sins plus presents sins. God will charge you from generation to generation for your sins 'if' you don't repent and ask his son 'Jesus Christ' forgiveness. Until you repent for the evil done to his people (black people) you can't be forgiven, by Jesus.

Despite seeing an unprecedented degree of black participation in American political life, Reconstruction was ultimately frustrating for African Americans, and the rebirth of white supremacy—including the rise of racist organizations such as the Ku Klux Klan (KKK)—had triumphed in the South by 1877.

Almost a century later, resistance to the lingering racism and discrimination in America that began during the slavery era would lead to the civil rights movement of the 1960s, which would achieve the greatest political and social gains for blacks since Reconstruction.

To show white people haven't repent their sins (God have charge you with those sins however). The Republicans are still trying to deny God's people a sample human right (the right to vote), Republicans keep trying to change the voting laws 'or' how people vote (black people). When Republicans stand before God at the end of their lives, God ask them "how do you plead guilty or not-guilty", what will your answer be? There you can't lie (God already knows the answer). "You shall be judged", so says God.

Because black people had to fight for the right to be free, they were freed to do what (with what). The land they had work all their lives (they were kicked off) with nowhere to go. Most went back into slavery just to be able to live (share cropping) another name for slavery.

FREEDOM, something we all feel today (something if taken away) we would give all we own to get it back. This is what the white man did to black people (God's people) for over 400 years only they couldn't get it back. God said, "repent and atone your sins".

Even people in jail can dream of a day when freedom will come (white people took that away from black people for over 400 years) and that's plain evil. Only people of the Devil could do that. "Whom shall ye serve"? So says God.

Black people were put on auction blocks sold off like animals. If that wasn't bad enough evil white people would inspect them like a horse for their plantations needs. If it was a breeding plantation they chose the best one's for breeding. They did this by inspecting their private parts (think of that). Smelly white men with theirs hands all over young black slave girls, boys, women, and men.

White people use this as a form of entertainment (watching blacks mate) as you would a horse. White people used slaves for all kinds of things, work hands, sex toys, and someone to abuse when they become bored. Black slaves were the most valuable product that white people owned (they could be used for everything) then be sold like a horse for profit.

White people that owned slaves didn't have to be very smart (too become rich) 'If' they had slaves and land (that was enough) the slaves did the rest. The slaves did all the work, made more slaves, and could be sold for other needs. What product today is that valuable? Now you can see why white people fought so hard to keep it (slaves). A product like slaves on the stock market today would be worth more than gold 'or' sliver 'or' anything else.

The color of a man's skin don't make the man only man do that. God said, "All my children can come unto me by way of my son Jesus Christ". So white people all people are God's people (even you). "Choose ye this day whom ye shall serve", so says God.

V.

THIS WILL GIVE WHITE people of today at look at what it was like before slavery and the aftermath. Close your eyes, now think of someone being shackled (like sardines in a can), next to each other (no room to move), having to relieve yourself (on yourself), having to eat in the same place (the dark hole of a ship) for over 6 months.

Now open your eyes, because your mind can't even think of something so evil. But this is just one of the things white people did to black people (they did things much worst) for over 400 years. Now say you're not the Devil.

When black people arrived in America as slaves (the one's that lived that is) they were then herded like cattles, put on auction blocks, and sold like animals. Sold to white people that would make the rest of their lives a living HELL. This was the work of the Devil (white people) against God's people (black people). God charge your whole race until all white people repent and make atonement for their sins.

This is when the separations of families all begin (now the same thing is happen today). Because the same kind of people that did it then are the same kind of people during it today (the Devil's people).

Because black people are still fighting for the rights to vote, something that was supposed to have been settled with voting rights. So, God sent an angel to fight this fight, his name was Martin L. King. Now the fight for the rights of black people can began (God has send his own people).

A man called by God to serve him, Martin Luther King, Jr., original name Michael King, Jr., (born January 15, 1929, Atlanta, Georgia, U.S.—died April 4, 1968, Memphis, Tennessee), Baptist minister and social activist who led the civil rights movement in the United States from the mid-1950s until his death by assassination in 1968.

Martin lived the life of a middle-class family, his father was a pastor, and his father was a pastor. He grew up in the church and soon became a pastor himself. God gave Martin a voice that commanded attention.

Because of the segregation in the south, King saw at a very young age the in-differents of the races in the south.

So, after graduating from college King was committed to fighting for racial inequality.

King then started a nu-violent movement to fight for the cause of racial injustice. He marched throughout the south while being beaten, disrespected, and jailed. His march on Washington was so powerful it forces congress to enact the Civil Rights Act.

With the Civil Rights Act, King had started something so powerful that it inspired a movement that change the laws for black people, causing Congress to enacted the Civil Rights Act in 1964, the same year King himself was honored with the Nobel Peace Prize. Posthumously awarded the Presidential Medal of Freedom, King is an icon of the civil rights movement. His life and work symbolize the quest for equality and nondiscrimination that lies at the heart of the American—and human—dream.

To this day, Martin's speech "I have a dream" is one of the most powerful speeches every made. God had shown him the future (same as Moses) only this time God's people get there before Martin.

Now, all white people should know that all other people dreams, hurts, sufferings, and needs are the same as theirs. Unless that people is the Devil's people. Because the Devil don't care who he hurts 'or' make suffer.

Then, God sent angel #2 from the north (people tried to say he was a violent man) his name was "Malcolm X, just because he said, "by any means necessary".

He was called Detroit Red before becoming (Malcolm X), he was born Malcolm Little on May 19, 1925 in Omaha, Nebraska. His mother, Louise Norton Little, was a homemaker occupied with the family's eight children. His father, Earl Little, was an outspoken Baptist minister and avid supporter of Black Nationalist leader Marcus Garvey.

Malcolm came from the streets of the motor city, he was a pimp, and con man. He was convicted of wrong doings and sent to prison. There he met a person form the Muslin brotherhood. He starting studying the ways of the Muslin fate.

When Malcolm was released from prison, he join the Muslin fate. He soon became the spoke person for the Muslin brotherhood.

Some of his many other goals, the NOI fought for a state of their own, separate from one inhabited by white people. By the time he was paroled in 1952, Malcolm was a devoted follower with the new surname "X" (He considered "Little" a slave name and chose the "X" to signify his lost tribal name.).

Then Malcolm would found out something about his mentor "Elijah Muhammad". After his special on TV, Malcolm was faced with the uncomfortable reality that his fame had eclipsed that of his mentor Elijah Muhammad. In addition to the media, Malcolm's vivid personality had captured the government's attention. As membership in the NOI continued to grow, FBI agents infiltrated the organization (one even acted as Malcolm's bodyguard) and secretly placed bugs, wiretaps, cameras, and other surveillance equipment to monitor the group's activities.

In knowing what he knew (Malcolm's faith was dealt a crushing blow) this was at the height of the civil rights movement in 1963. He learned that his mentor and leader, Elijah Muhammad, was secretly having relations with as many as six women within the Nation of Islam organization. As if that were not enough, Malcolm found out that some of these relationships had resulted in children.

AFTER Malcolm went to Mecca on a pilgrimage his ideas about white people changed. He no longer saw all white people as the Devil. Malcolm was able to walk and pray with white people. He saw them as no different than any other Muslim. As I stated before (not all white people are the Devil) now Malcolm see the same thing. So, when he returned to America (Malcolm's) views had changed about white people.

After his return from Mecca, knowing what he knew about Muhammad, and Malcolm's change in view point about white people (he knew his time on earth wasn't long). The same as Jesus, as Martin, and now Malcolm. All 3 knew their deaths were coming, this will be their sacrifice for man-kind. After Malcolm's death Harlem showed it's love.

Because all of Harlem loved him, Malcolm was known as the Prince of Harlem, Fifteen hundred people attended Malcolm's funeral in Harlem on February 27, 1965 at the Faith Temple Church of God in Christ (now Child's Memorial Temple Church of God in Christ). After the ceremony, friends took the shovels away from the waiting gravediggers and buried Malcolm themselves.

These were 2 angels sent from God as a sacrifice for his people (black people) 'so' black people don't let it be for nothing. Now, black people get up, go out then register (if you're not), and then vote. 展e know not what hour or second so says God. What we do know is that this person (Donald Trump) the Devil must be removed from the White House.

Dr. King was an angel with a voice sent from God when he spoke people had to listen and Malcolm X was an angel like Jesus, from the lest of us, he became the best of us.

The Devil have taken 2 of God's angels and now he will send angel #3 (with the power of God). Now white people be ware, this angel will not be a sacrifice for man, but have the power of God behind him.

White people claimed they discovered American but the Indian was here first (the only true American) is the

Indian. The white man took his land and put the Indian on a reservation. Then called the Indian a salvage when he fought to keep his land, and a victory when white men killed them to take it away.

Look how white people use words to make the word (black) an evil word. Everything bad starts with black, Black Friday, Black Sunday, and of course Black Man. The white people want you to see black as evil the opposite to white as good that's how the Devil showed it to them. This is how God showed it to his people (after the darkness comes the light). God said, "I am the light follow me out of the darkness into the light". So, now black people all you have to do is be the opposite of darkness them you will see the light.

The KKK, a bunch of cowardly white men with white sheets over their faces (trying to hide their evil during s). You can't hide from God (he sees, knows, everything) 'so' now repent ask Jesus forgiveness, and God will save you. "Choose ye this day" so says God.

This is the first time white people used something white as a sign of evil I guess they didn't like black sheets (since everything else bad start with black).

The white man have claimed everything he came in contact with as his own, 'so' claiming American was no different. Since you couldn't enslave the Indian to work the land (you took it). You enslaved your own people first. After that enslaving black people was a cake walk. Now the white man would have free labor for the next 400 years.

So, if you think you are not the Devil (white people) think again. However you can escape the Devil, 'by' confessing your sins, and asking the Lord Jesus Christ "forgiveness".

Again the Devil (white people) use the Bible for over 400 years to keep black people (God's people) enslaved.

After King and Malcolm was killed it started a movement that gained great advances for the cause of black people. Black people where now able to secure the right to vote, and get black people elected to higher position in government.

The train for equal rights for black people was now moving in the right directions. The doors of opportunity where now kicked wide open (black people were excelling in everything).

Before professional sports became 90% black it was just a white man's hobby. Now that black players dominate all 3 sports they have become muti-billion dollars businesses. Still not one black person own a football, basketball, or baseball team (I forgot one person own a basketball team).

These sports teams (NFL, NBA) are nothing more than a plantation with high prices slaves working on it. When you can be sold, traded, and told what to say (you're a high price slave period). Now stop allowing them to control your freedom of speech. God gave you special talents for a reason (not just to play sports) start using it to speak out against in-justice. "You will be judge" so says God.

When a black player standup for the cause of blackness then all other black players should support him (you have the power). Black players are 90% of all 3 major professional sports with 1% ownership. Black players are the product that make it all work (with no ownership) something is wrong with that picture. Start using your power, stop letting the white masters control you (without you they have nothing). Start demanding ownership, stop being high paid slaves making the masters even richer (you have the power) use it.

Your talents came from God (not the white masters) now start during what God gifted you for (not just to play ball) 'but' to standup for the cause of blackness. "You too will be judged" so says God.

Now all you black ball players, actors, and artists that have been so very, very blessed by God should start standing up for the cause of blackness (your gifts came from God) you will be judged.

God gifted you so you can serve his people (black people), God's people (your people). Now stop abandanting them when they need you after you have become successful. Because God is the reason why you're successful. God said, "Whom shall ye serve"?

God sent his angels to earth to protect man so that he wouldn't have to destroy the earth again for the sins of man.

"Because of my angels on earth, I will not destroy man again, I will not sacrifice another angel, evil will not rule", so says God.

Twice the Devil tried to enslave God's people, the third time God sent an angel, "Barack Obama". No one saw him coming (only God knew) he had to keep it from the Devil.

VI. God sent an angel to spearhead his army "Barack Obama"

❧❦❧

GOD ALLOW HIS ONLY son to die on the cross for the sins of man. All man have to do too become saved is ask his son "Jesus Christ" forgiveness and be saved by God. Still man choose the Devil (look at the world today), 'if' you though the answer was "no".

Then God sent someone that American didn't see coming, 'to' try to bring his children back from the Devil. That someone was named, "Barack Obama".

Just like Jesus, "Barack Obama" was the lest of us 'to' become the best of us.

God sent this angel, 'Barack Obama', in full Barack Hussein Obama II, (born August 4, 1961, Honolulu, Hawaii, U.S.), 44th president of the United States (2009–17) and the first African American to hold the office. Before winning the presidency, Obama represented Illinois in the U.S. Senate (2005–08). He was the third African American to be elected to that body since the end of Reconstruction (1877). In 2009 he was awarded the Nobel Peace Prize "for his extraordinary efforts to strengthen international diplomacy and cooperation between peoples."

Obama's family is the perfect example of what a God loving family should be. Just look at his loving wife, and his 2 lovely daughters. This is the example God wants his people to 'see' then you will know it was God that sent him. A righteous man showing God's people how to live a righteous life. "Choose ye this day", so says God.

After the nomination for president was won, Barrack Obama had to choose his running mate 'Joseph R. Biden Jr'. Joe Biden had been a U.S. senator from Delaware since 1972, was a one-time Democratic candidate for president and served as chairman of the Senate Foreign Relations Committee. Obama's opponent was long-time Arizona Senator John S. McCain, a Vietnam veteran and former prisoner-of-war, who chose Alaska Governor Sarah Palin as his running mate. If elected, Palin would have been the nation's first-ever female vice-president.

WITH only a short time left, most polls showed Obama as the front-runner. Sadly, Obama's maternal grandmother, Madelyn Dunham, died after a battle with cancer on November 3, the day before voters went to the polls. She had been a tremendously influential force in her grandson's life and had diligently followed his historic run for office from her home in Honolulu.

AFTER WINNING, Obama spoke to America, he said, "we may not get there in one year or even one term, but America, I have never been more hopeful than I am tonight that we will get there. I promise you, we as a people will get there".

Barack Obama was the first African-American to not only be nominated by a major party but also to win the presidency of the United States. He ran as an agent of change. His true impact and the significance of his presidency will not be determined for many years to come.

With the election of the first black president, 'Barack Obama' it cause an uprising among white people. White people (the Devil) started gathering their army. The war between good (God) and evil (the Devil) will be held in the sea of politics.

The elections of a black person as president drove white people crazy, they couldn't have dreamed this in their worst nightmare. White people didn't think black people could do anything but pick cotton 'or' make babies. After the election of a blackman a lot of white people had to be put on suicide watch.

So, the shock of a blackman as the leader of the free world, almost drove them mad. Any time half the government can say, "our job is to make Barack Obama a one turn president", just because he is black (something is wrong with that picture).

When the election is over and a winner has been decided (a fair election that is), then the country supposed to come together as Americans (period)!

But after the election of the first black president, the Devil alone with (the help from the Bible, the Russians) was able to trick people and win the election for president (now the Devil is in the White House).

Before Moses had to use the power of God to force Pharoah to let his people go, now God have to convince the people to let the Devil go.

The Devils army has now showed its hand (the Devil found his leader), Donald Trump. The war has now begun. The lines have now been drawn. Americans can no longer sit on the side line 'or' on the fence. It's time to act, register, and vote.

Remember you can't bargain with the Devil (he will cut the baby in-half) he has to be destroyed on earth. Once Donald Trump is powerless the Devil will abandon him. Then he will return to HELL to wait on another Donald

Trump, we as 'Americans' must make sure that never happens again.

This is a message to all people that follow Donald Trump, 'Your time has come and gone', 'the future you seek will never be again� so says God.

Even before Obama was elected as the first black president, black people had made major stripes in politic. The first black governor of a southern state, the first black mayor of a major city, and many more blacks being elected to congress.

Black people have achieved more in the last 100 years than any other race on earth. From slavery to the highest office in the land (the President of the United States of America), "the lest of us will become the greatest of us" so says God.

The city that Donald Trump keep bad mouthing (Chicago) because that's where Obama got his start, have now elected its first black woman mayor (she brought the light), the chief of police is black, and the attorney general is black (a woman), so say what you want about Chicago, "it's black controlled now". Because black power is voting power and that's the power that works. "The bottom rail shall be the top rail and top rail shall be the bottom rail", so says God.

When Trump use Chicago as an element of violent s (although there is a lot of violent s their) from people without hope, coming from a president that don't care, what's the point. This is a man that keeps breaking the laws he was elected to up-hold and all the Republicans that allow him to keep during it, history first then God will judge you later.

Donald Trump is not a King "or' Dictator, someday he will be out of office. If not sooner then later. What will you do then? When someone else is president and start making their own laws, what will you say then? What actions will you take then? When you sell all your values and soul to the Devil there is no re-fund. HELL will be your final home. God said, "You can't serve 2 masters".

VII. Now the Devil is in the White House, "Donald Trump"

⸙

THE DEVIL WAS HERE from the beginning, ever since he persuaded Eve to eat fruit from the forbidding tree. Man cause God to reject the Bible, 'by' using it in his name to justfly all the wrong things they do. The Bible is still the greatest book ever written. It still contains the words of God, 'but' only Godly people will be able to determine the difference. So, keep reading the Bible, 'but' be very careful of the words you read (it maybe the Devil specking).

The Devil waited until the right person came along, somebody without a soul, empty, hollow, greedy, selflessness, and void of anything (Donald Trump) to head his army.

The Devil has been gathering his army since the beginning of time, now he found someone to lead it. The Devil was here before "Jesus Christ".

Would God put his name on anything that the Devil take an oath on everyday? The Bible.

All these people that follow Donald Trump go to church and read from the Bible, who words do they hear? The Devil.

Look at all these white racist groups, the 'KKK' or the 'Skin Heads' all hate groups, and all white groups. These people (white people) that like to burn and hang God's people. Only demons of the Devil could do that. No other human person could burn another human person unless that person was completely evil (demons) of the Devil.

White people have never invented anything meaningful to the world, except control. When other races invent it, white people just stamp their names on it, then take it. They stand on the shoulders of other races and profit from their inventions.

Look at what white people took from black people (Booker T. Wasthington), the Chineses, and most of all the Indian. They took their land and claimed it as their own (America). God created the earth for all people, 'so' white people stop trying to play God (the job is taken).

When your time on this earth is up, you will take nothing with you. Then you will have to stand before Jesus asking for forgiveness, there you will see the error of your ways, and the sentence will be, "you will reap what you soy", so says God.

The violent and racist ways of (white people) cause their souls to be dark, leaving the door open for these demons to enter, once inside they grew stronger, causing them to become more evil, and then do the bidding for the Devil.

Once the Devil start using you (you neglect your body) your body start to become repulseable (look at Trump), see how much different he looked 10 years ago. Look at what happen to "Elvis" he sold his soul to the Devil for music he stole from black musicians, see what happen to his body, and then he killed himself. The Devil had no more use for him then abandon him (a lost soul). The same thing will happen to "Donald Trump" and all people that follow him..

Now that the leader for the Devils army has been born "Donald Trump" who was born on June 14, 1946, in Queens, New York, the Devil had been waiting on him ever since the beginning of time.

This is a man that think money is everything, 'so' his so called Net Worth according to a September 2017 Forbes estimate, Donald Trump's net worth is $3.1 billion. Of that, $1.6 billion is in New York real estate; $570 million is in golf clubs and resorts; $500 million is in non-New York real estate; $290 million is in cash and personal assets; and $200 million is in brand businesses.

What kind of man who brag about his many women (to the world), 'this man' Donald J. Trump was married three other times and is currently married to Slovenian model Melania Knauss (now Trump), over 23 years his junior. In January 2005, the couple married in a highly-publicized and lavish wedding.

To show how bigger lie re Trump is, some of the people he claim to hate today was at his wedding. Among the many celebrity guests at the wedding were Hillary Clinton and former President Bill Clinton.

Remember the day Trump came down an escalator and declared his nomination for president. No one believed he had a chance in HELL. What a word to say about the Devil (HELL) his home. When he began his political career by seeking the nomination for the Reform Party for the 2000 presidential race and withdrew; he again publicly announced he would be running for president in the 2012 election.

To everyone s surprise Trump was able to beat all the other field of Republicans running for president. However it wasn't until the 2016 election that Trump became the official Republican nominee for president and, defying polls and media projections, won the majority of electoral college votes in a stunning victory on November 8, 2016. So, despite losing the popular vote to Hillary Clinton by almost 2.9 million votes, Trump's electoral win—306 votes to Clinton's 232 votes — clinched his election as the 45th president of the United States.

So, something nobody saw coming against impossible odds, and one of the most contentious presidential races in U.S. history, Trump's rise to the office of president was considered a resounding rejection of establishment politics by blue-collar and working class Americans. In his victory speech, Trump said: "he pledge to every citizen of our land that I will be president for all Americans." About his supporters, he said: "ours was not a campaign, but rather an incredible and great movement made up of millions of hard-working men and women who love their country and want a better, brighter future for themselves and for their families". Now you see this man for what he is (a lie re and a con man)

Since you have read about 2 presidents, their values, and their sense of honor (who will you serve)?

Now that you have seen how the Devil use the Bible to persuade, be very careful of the things you read (it maybe the Devil specking).

When the largest platforms in the world (Facebook, Twitter) can be used to send out false information to influence the outcome of a presidential election and lie about it (it should be dis-banded) any other company would be. The owners sold their souls to the Devil for power and money. They should be indicted same as all the other Rats. But if you think you have gotten away (think again), God will judge you later.

This is the final conflict (it will be fought in the sea of politics), 'so' get up, get out, register, and vote.

Everyday the fires of HELL keeps getting hotter and hotter for this (White House) soon it will go up in flames, Republican Party are you willing to burn in HELL, for Donald Trump?

This is the future for
all man-kind
"Which house do you choose"?
the
Devil's House 'or' God's House

VIII. The Devil's house (the Republican Party)

❦

THE DEVIL WAS THE Ark-Angel, he sat next to God in heaven, he was the most powerful of all God's angels. MISUSE OF POWER is what lead to his being exiled from Heaven. The Devil once sat at the right side of God (how could something so right go so wrong?), one word "POWER". The Devil made the mistake of challenging God in heaven (who's power is almighty power), and was kicked out. You would think the Devil would learn from his mistakes but "no" here the Devil (Donald Trump) is on earth making the same mistakes again.

There have always been wars through-out history about good versus evil (good always win) because good is about the truth and the truth will always over take a lie. Evil is always based on lies, mores lies, and more lies to cover up the first lie. Now we have a president (Donald Trump) that's the perfect fit, to the Devil's plan.

I should know the Devil (that's why God chose me to write this) because I was once him. God saved me from the Devil '3' times (the 3rd time) God made me know it was him. God said, "Whom shall ye serve", he showed me whom to serve, and it was him (God).

The Devil waited until the right person came along, somebody without a soul, empty, hollow, greedy, selflessness, and void of anything (Donald Trump) to head his army. The Devil has been gathering his army since the beginning of time, now he found someone to lead it. The Devil was here before "Jesus Christ" LYING IN WAITING.

Think about this, would God truly back anything that the Devil take an oath on everyday? The Bible.

All these people that follow Donald Trump go to church and read words from the Bible, who words do they hear? The Devil's.

When Trump can say, "If I shoot someone on 5th Ave. I wouldn't lose any support" and people keep wondering why? These people are the offsprings of the demons as I said before. Only a people that evil could except something like that (that is so evil). As long, as Trump is their leader they will follow him even to HELL. Because HELL is their home that is where Satan lives.

Donald Trump was born on June 14, 1946, in Queens, New York, the Devil had been waiting on him since the beginning of time.

His so called Net Worth according to a September 2017 Forbes estimate, Donald Trump's net worth is $3.1 billion. Of that, $1.6 billion is in New York real estate; $570 million is in golf clubs and resorts; $500 million is in non-New York real estate; $290 million is in cash and personal assets; and $200 million is in brand businesses. That's down from $3.7 billion in 2016, according to Fortune, mostly due to declining New York real estate values. Only the Devil think money is the keys to the kingdom of heaven

ALL, the so called people of God that follow Donald Trump (the Devil) will end up in HELL with him. God is a jealous (God), he said "put no other God before me" now you're putting the Devil before him.

God also said, "You can't serve 2 masters" 'so' now choose what master you will serve (God or the Devil).

Mitch McConnell said after the election of the first black president 'Barack Obama; "his job was to make Obama a one turn President" No, your job was to serve the American people. That meant all the people not the few for the Devil (you will be judged) later, to ask Jesus forgiveness. What will you say?

Obama won the president-est by a land side that meant most Americans agreed with his politics. Then the Republican Party decided to divide the country even after the people had spoken. Wins only count when they win, no matter how they win. Both wins for president they lost the popular vote (the voice of the people) they won in questionable decisions. This was not the will of most Americans.

This is the weakest leader the Republican Party everyone had, Paul Davis Ryan Jr. is an American politician serving since 2015 as the 54th Speaker of the United States House of Representatives. He was the 2012 vice presidential nominee of the Republican Party, running alongside former Massachusetts Governor Mitt Romney

Both these (followers of the Devil) tried for 8 years, all of Obama's time as president to appeal and replace (Obama care). They didn't say what it would be replace with, just that they were going to replace it. The republicans voted to appeal it many, many times when Obama was in office.

However, after they won all 3 branches of government, they couldn't get the job done. Something they had done many, many times when it didn't count. That should tell you something about their ability to govern.

However Democrats could bolster the law with additional financial assistance or simply replace it with a straightforward government insurance program, Republicans would ratchet back the regulations, cut funding for Medicaid and provide less assistance to the poor. "The meek shall inherit the earth" so says God.

Paul Davis Ryan Jr, sold his soul to the Devil for nothing. He betrayed all his believes for someone without any morals, honor, or duty to country. When you sell your soul to the Devil there are no refunds just the fires of HELL after that. However you can prevent that by asking Jesus forgiveness and returning to the house of God.

When Obama was president, Paul Ryan was a deficit hawk, now the deficit is 3 times higher under the Republican Party leadership (his leadership). What a bunch of lairs. Everything they object to when Obama was president is 'OK' now, like the tax bill that was supposed to help poor people but made the richer (richer).

So many taxpayers wonder about tax changes now that reform is the law. Your high-net-worth clients have special questions.

This year along the government is expected to borrow more than a trillion dollars in the coming year, in part to make up for tax receipts that have been slashed by GOP tax cuts.

Now that corporate tax collections fell by 31 percent in the fiscal year ending Sept. 30, despite robust corporate profits. That's hardly surprising after lawmakers cut the corporate tax rate from 35 percent to 21.

When McConnell's made a statement, his comments drew a swift rebuke from the top Democrat in the Senate, Chuck Schumer, D-N.Y., who blamed the rising deficit on Republicans' "tax cut for the rich."

Each year the deficit typically grows during recessions — when tax receipts shrink and demand for food stamps and other government assistance rises — then falls during good times

Sometimes the current spike in the deficit at a time of strong economic growth and low unemployment represents a break with that historical pattern.

The last time unemployment was this low was in 1969 and the federal government ran a small surplus.

Since peaking at nearly 10 percent of GDP in 2009, the deficit declined as share of the economy through 2015. It's been rising since, hitting 3.9 percent of GDP in the fiscal year just ended.

Now you know (you been lie to), Paul Ryan is a hypocrite, and the tax bill make the richer (richer). Come to a party you can trust, the Democratic Party.

After the Democrats won the House in a land side, it shock the Devil. Now he knows (he's in trouble). This is making him do all kinds of crazy things, sending all kinds of crazy messages. No one knows what he saying from one day to the next.

Now that the pressure is on, Trump may crack at any second. You want someone like that the leader of the free world (at lest that's the way it supposed to be) until the election of the Devil, "Donald Trump".

SOMEONE, that govern on a whim (I heard something that sounded good at the time) most fuck ups sounded good at the time. Are you willing to risk the future of your kids on that?

Now that Mueller have found Trump of wrong doing even if he can't be locked up (something they wanted to happen too Hillary) is now happening to them. All the 'RATS' have left the ship except the Republican Party, I guess they're willing to go down with the ship

When all the law enforcement's of America (FBI, CIA, DOJ) have said that the Russia meddled in the presidential election (the Republics know all this) but don't care, and the only people saying it didn't happen is Donald Trump (the Devil) on one shore, Putin (the Devil) on the other shore. From one shore (to one shore) the battle for 'good' verses 'evil' in the sea of politics. "Whom will ye serve"? So says God.

When you sell your soul to the Devil, there is no refund, it's a soul that will burn in HELL for ever. Is Donald Trump worth that? He wouldn't do it for you. If you follow the Devil to HELL it's too late (God can't save you) from HELL.

All of his Rats have pleaded guilty and made a deal with Mueller. But the Republican Party still stand with this president that have done impeachable offenses. What do this man have over the Republican Party that they are willing to destroy their future and lose their souls to the Devil?

This was about the Russian's messing around in our elections, something if Obama was accused of during the Republican Party would want him tried for treason and hung. Something the Devil loved during to God's people for over 500 years, 400 as slaves, another 100 just because they loved hanging black people (God's people).

A Russian national who claimed ties to the Kremlin told President Trump's personal attorney, Michael Cohen, as early as November 2015 that he could use his Russian government connections to help Trump's business and political prospects.

They said he was also able to provide information about contacts with White House officials after Trump took office and the circumstances that surrounded the preparation of his false testimony to Congress.

It is January 1, 2019 the Devil is in the White House, the Democracy party just won the house. Now they're coming after the Devil.

Republican party is it worth loosing your soul to the Devil for something that is meanessly in heaven (to God)?

"JESUS CHRIST or the ANTICHRIST... WHOSE SIDE ARE YOU ON"?

WE ARE NEARING THE MIDNIGHT HOUR...We don't know the DAY or the HOUR, but it is clearly IMMINENT!

"Choose you this day whom ye shall serve...", so says God.

Remember Satan will gather his army from one shore (Russia) to one shore (Unity State of America) then the battle for all mankind will be held in the sea of politics. The Devil can't win, 'so' please! Please!! Register, and vote.

"A rich man has as much changes of getting to heaven as a camel jumping through the eye of a needle" so says God.

Republicans don't sell your soul for something (money) the Devils perfect weapon, and will be the fuels for the fires of HELL.

You're following a man (the Devil) that is all about money when you follow him it will take you straight to HELL.

"When you reap what you soy (seen the error of your ways) you will end up in 'Heaven or HELL.

Now I'm as mad as the mad man in the white house. I'm a Vietnam veteran that faced combat in Vietnam, I was almost killed by a VC Terrorist in face to face combat which I was able to kill him. The Republican Party is now allowing this man that didn't even serve 'or' visit the troops in combat made combat decisions on his own. The party that supposed to be fiscal responsible and support the military (what a bunch of liars).

71

This is how history will remember the Republican Party. But don't worry your time will be up soon and God will judge you after that.

The Republican's knew Trump was an idiot 'but' they thought they could control him. They knew he would sign any bill they could send him 'but' they couldn't even get their act together, now he is an out-of-control idiot that they can't control. So, now it's up to the Democrats to put him in check.

When Republican try to defend this president when every word coming out of his mouth is a lie and still have a straight face during so (something is wrong with them). Donald Trump have turned all Republicans that follow him into children of the Devil. If you want to burn in Hell 'or' spent forever in darkness trying to escape the demons of HELL keep following Donald Trump. Time to decide, God said "you can't serve 2 masters".

Some ex-Republicans are always talking about truth to power "Is there someone that can speck it to Trump"? Yes, God is now that someone (his truth is the truth) and his power (is almighty power).

God created the earth for all his children not the chosen few by man, what give one man (Donald Trump) the right to make that chose? Remember long ago one man though he was a God (God showed him he wasn't) now here's another man thinking he's a king, remember what happen to that king.

So, now this want-to-be king is during the same thing, remember what happen to his people. When he's willing to shut down the government for his own ego and make million suffer, and the people that allow it to happen will also pay. "You can't serve 2 masters" so says God.

Donald Trump act like America is his alone (the Indian was here all the time) black man had been to America long before white man came. When Donald Trump and all white people trace their roots back to the beginning they will find a (black man). Because a black man was the first man on earth (period)! God said, "From the earth we came to the earth we will return". The earth is make of dark soil.

The Indians was here all the time, the black man came taught the Indians ancient ways, and left. The white man came later acting like he discovered it, then name it, and claim it. God was here first, the Indian 2nd, and the black man 3rd. Now this small man (Donald Trump) with a big ego is acting like America belong to white people only. "The meek shall inherit the earth" so says God.

EGO, such a small word that fit such a small man (Donald Trump). Someone that would look weak next to a first grader. So, Republican Party that should show you how weak you are going forth.

Trump couldn't get the votes for his WALL when the Republicans controlled all 3 branches of government. So, why would he thank he could get it with the Democrats controlling the House? This was the Devil causing thousands of people to *suffer for nothing. God will judge you for this, when you allow the Devil to cause his people to suffer needless.*

Republicans the Devil have taken over your party (Donald Trump) someone who has abandon God. When the Devil is finish with him (the Devil will abandon him to) then his soul will become a (lost soul) too wonder forever in darkness trying to escape the demons of HELL (there is no escape). Following this man will cause your soul to end up like that (I know you don't want that).

Then, there's these 2 white women s that are standing before the cameras lying for Donald Trump with the appearance of the white wick witches of the west 'or' just as evil has he is. God will judge you for that and the Devil will abandon you after that. Then you will become (a lost soul) to wonder in darkness forever trying to escape the demons of HELL. Because Jesus don't forgive and God don't save the Devil's rejects.

Because all Republicans know that (Putin) help (Donald Trump) win the election for president. He is to stupid too have done it on his own now Trump's in Putin's pocket for the election and many other things. So, when Putin say jump, Trump say, "which way and how far". God said, "who will ye serve".?

Trump had meetings with Putin that only 'he' Putin and his people know about what was said. When ask Trump gave a long speech but never said during that speech the word 'NO', If a question is ask with a yes 'or' no answer the answer should be one or the other not a long speech saying nothing. The reason Trump didn't say 'NO' he though Putin maybe listening to his answer. What more will it take to make Republicans see the light?

The Republicans that are letting Trump trash the rule of law and looking the other way, history will record this. What lie will you tell your grandchildren? When they ask what you did to up hold the law. When you were against everything Obama did and said 'but' except things much worst that Trump have said, and done. You will be judge by history 'but' most of all by God.

All people (of all races) who are nu-decided that may be forgiven by Jesus and saved by God 'or' not evil enough to be chosen by the Devil (souls will be lost). You know what happens to lost souls. God said, "I am the light". "Chose ye this day" so says God.

God said, "Put no other God before me". Remember the flood. God is a jealous God. You don't want to angry him. That's why he sent Jesus as a go between, all you have to do is repent the sins to his people, ask is son forgiveness, and God will save you.

So, all white preachers that are spooking the word of God much know until you repent for over 500 years of sins to his people (you have no right to speck his name). The same Bible you are using today (you use it to keep God's people enslaved for over 400 years).

Now, Democratic when you take back control of the house, don't rush to impeach. Remember the old saying, "give a man enough rope he'll hang himself" if this don't work the 3rd and *final wave will. The Devil has to be destroyed on earth in order to be sent back to HELL.*

Then his army will go back in hiding powerless. Because these people will always follow the Devil, they are the demons of Satan (that was kicked out of heaven). That's the reason no matter what Trump says 'or' do, they will still follow him, after all he's their leader, the Devil (Donald Trump).

Another thing, all these so called religious people that's following the Devil (Donald Trump) someone who said, "when someone do something to me I do 10 times back to them" this is called revenge. "Vengeance is mine" says the Lord. You will be judged harshly. God said, "You can't follow the Devil and believe in me". Now God will send wave, after wave, and after wave to right the ship.

The first wave took the House, the second wave will take the Senate, and the 3rd wave will take back the White House. "The Republican Party will be no more", so says God. This will destroy the Devil on earth and send him back to HELL.

Most Republicans read the BIBLE claim to know God but follow the Devil (Donald Trump). God said, "You can't serve 2 masters". Your party is becoming like a city in the Bible that was so full of sin until God had to destroy it. Only this time there is no family without sin, 'no' reason for God to wait. God said, "Choose ye this day".

When you have lived pass 70 years of age "God's promise" then you have been bless by God. Your soul have been saved 'it's' up to you to lose it. So why are all these white people in congress over 70 years of age losing their soul to the Devil? When he finish with you, the Devil (Donald Trump) will abandon you (you can't go back to God) your soul will become a lost soul. "Whom will ye serve?" God is asking you.

It is now January 8, 2019 the last day for time to go in so people effected by the shut-down to get paid (they want get paid) the government is still shut-down for nothing (a WALL). Now the news networks are allowing the Devil to use their platform to lie to all of Americans. They denied Barack Obama use for what they said was politically reasons now they let a compulsively liar (lie to all Americans), God will judge you for that.

Trump met with Democrats to reopen the government but because he couldn't get his way through a temp tantrum like a spoil child and walk out. Then said the Democrats shutdown the government (the world saw him on TV saying he was glad to shutdown government) now all his crones from the vice-president on down is telling the same lie as if they didn't watch him saying it on TV. All of them was there. What's wrong with all these people that they will lie and know they are lying for Donald Trump?

BECAUSE, the truth never changes 'but' Trump's lies keep changing from one day to the next. How can Republicans keep a straight face defending him (unless they are the Devil) to? "You can't serve 2 masters", so says God.

The networks alone with the vice-president (Pence) and the white house is using a national platform to allow Donald Trump to lie to the World (history will remember this) what lie will you tell your children in future? When they can read the truth and then read what you did.

Now Trump is between a rock and hard place (playing Russian-roulette) with 2 bullets in the chamber, one from the Russians, the other one from Mueller. If Trump loses, he lose the support of his army (the Devils army) then he make be shot by both bullets. Democratic s, Trump is fighting for his life (he will do anything). "The Devil shall not win", so says God.

Now both parties The Democratic s and The Republicans should do their jobs and let Donald Trump do his (which is nothing). They should pass bills that help the people that sent them to congress in the first place, force Trump to sign 'or' veto (put the ball square in his court) then override his veto, 'if' he refuse to sign. I said before you can't bargain with The Devil (he'll cut the baby in-half). You have to take away all his chose s and force his hand. "Choose ye this day", so says God.

Stop acting like you are powerless when a mad man is in-charge of the fate of America, and the future of your children. God said, "You will be judged".

Another thing, stop trying to explain (Donald Trump), he's the Devil that's all you need to know, and everybody that follow him will end up in HELL. "Whom will you serve"? So says God.

Everybody should have seen Donald Trump coming at lest all God's people should have. Remember what happen to the fall of the Roman Empire when one man convince the people that he alone could fix their problems. When we remove God from anything the Devil takes over. People removed God from politics (now the Devil is in the White House) they removed God from schools now they're being shot-up (our children or no longer safe in school). God said, "I am the light".

Donald Trump have never degraded 'or' disrespected (Nancy Patricia D' Alesandro Pelosi) by giving her an evil name. The Devil know s when he's facing someone sent by God (the Devil can feel God's powers). 'Nancy Pelosi' is the first white person God chose to serve him after re-elevating woman. She chose God long ago 'so' he know s she's not one of them (demons). "Whom shall ye serve"? God know s whom she serves.

Now congress has the power to make the Devil (Donald Trump) powerless 'so' start during the will of the people instead of the bidding for the Devil. "You will be judged", so says God.

All these people Trump threw under the bus are now acting like they found God. You didn't act that way before (you can't fool God). God don't save the Devil's rejects, nuless they repent all their sins, and make complete atonement. Jesus said, "The way to the father is by me".

Now, Donald Trump keeping saying the Mueller investigations are a witch hunt (a lot of witches have been convicted or pleaded guilty in this hunt) now the dogs of the hunt have treed Trump, and his family.

His defense is being ignore of how the elections laws work (ignore he is) but being ignore is not a defense 'if' it was Trump would be innocent of everything. But all Americans know Trump did it (all except the Republican's), because they are the only one's now saying otherwise. This is from a man (Donald Trump) that said "only he could fix the problems of America" now he's claiming ignore (though he is ignore) but so are a lot of black people in jail today.

It makes you wonder, why would the Republican Party commit political suicide for Donald Trump? Unless the Russians have something on them to. God said, "You will be judged".

When the president has to be fact checked for every speech he gives, why would he be given a stage to lie to whole world (the State of the Union Address)? What a joke this country has become. Trump has make the greatest country in the world a joke, and laughing stock. History will remember this and all the people that in-able him. "Choose ye this day" so says God.

Now Trump is obsesses over a man after he's dead (John McCain) because he was a hero and Donald Trump was a coward. You can't change history. Because of that Trump can't let the dead rest in peace.

How sick can a person be? When they ask the dead to thank them for their own funeral, something every dead person get by being dead. That in itself would be the headlines of the century. A dead man thanking Trump for his funeral.

This sick man, leader of the free world (now) need to be replace as soon as possible. All these Republicans that is enabling this sick person will be judged by history, and then by God.

Trump is now trying to prove to himself that he has something that he don't (gusts). You can't bring back something you never had (you were a coward then) and you're still a coward now. Only now Trump is trying to prove it at the price of America. It's now time for ALL Americans to stand-up and say, "This is not America". This is no-longer about black 'or' white 'but' about what America we want our children to grow-up in.

When the Mueller report was finally finished, the top lawyer of the land, the AG (Barr) wrote a 4 page memo from a 400 page document clearing the president of any wrong doings. He made this decision all on his own, it wasn't what the 400 page document stated. The report supposed to go too congress for them to make that decision.

The AG supposed to be the head lawyer for all Americans, not to serve just the president (Donald Trump). So, why are these top people willing to destroy their career for Trump? History will remember this, 'but' God will judge you for this. You can't lie then, because God sees, hears, and know everything, "I'm the light of the world", so says God.

Now, come to truly know Jesus then you will see the light (God) and start going in the right directions. Your party is being led by the Devil in the wrong directions. I tried all my live to go with the Devil in the wrong direction 'but' God said, "no" he made me know him now my life is going in the right directions. People of the Republican party come to truly know God then you can no-longer follow the Devil (Donald Trump).

Donald Trump is obsessed with Barack Obama 'but' Obama was God sent, meaning the Devil can't touch 'so' Trump get over it. Because the power of God is almighty power. God removed the Devil from heaven the same way his people will remove Trump from the White House.

This is a final WARNING to all people that's on the fence (nu-decided) when death comes, and you are still nu-decided you will become one of those lost souls. The souls that's lost forever in darkness trying to escape the hounds of HELL, 'but' there is no escape. "Choose ye this day", so says God.

DEMOCRATIC

IX. God's house (the Democracy Party)

GOD ALLOW HIS ONLY son to die on the cross for the sins of man. All man have to do too become saved is ask his son "Jesus Christ" forgiveness and be saved by God. Still man chose the Devil (look at the world today), 'if' you though the answer was "no". Then God sent someone that American didn't see coming, 'to' try to bring his children back from the Devil. That someone was named, "Barack Obama".

This is a man sent by God to lead his army, Barack Obama, in full Barack Hussein Obama II, (born August 4, 1961, Honolulu, Hawaii, U.S.), 44th president of the United States (2009–17) and the first African American to hold that office. Before winning the presidency, Obama represented Illinois in the U.S. Senate (2005–08). He was the third African American to be elected to that body since the end of Reconstruction (1877). In 2009 he was awarded the Nobel Peace Prize "for his extraordinary efforts to strengthen international diplomacy and cooperation between peoples."

Obama was a 2 turn president that couldn't run a 3ʳᵈ time, otherwise he would be a 3 term president, so the Devil won the White House with the help from the Bible. The Devil use the Bible to persuade the ones that were nu-decided. The one's that say they believe in God but follow the Devil.

After losing the race for president that the democracy should have won, Donald Trump said, "they should have won". He didn't say, "The Russian help him win it".

Obama tried to warn Trump about the Russians meddling in the election (what a joke). He was telling the man that ask the Russians to meddle in the first place (about the Russians meddling).

Obama wanted the new elected president to be a success for the American people. He was pulling for him, so Obama stepped aside to get out of his way. He retired and did what all presidents before him have done (not bad mouth the president).

If, Obama had said one of the 100 things Trump said it would disqualify him as president. The Republicans would have voted to impeach Obama (if he had said) just one of Trump's remarks. Since Obama is a man sent by God (when the Republicans go low) God showed him how. God said, "I am the light".

Obama was able to embrace his opponent, people like John McCain, and George Bush. Even though they had different viewpoints. They were able to treat each other with respect.

Donald Trump who have never served anything but himself, called an American hero (not a hero) because he was captured. You have to be during something to be captured in the first place (fighting for his country) something Trump would know nothing about.

Now he's trying to act like a leader, Trump couldn't lead a horse to water. So, why are these people still with this mad man?

No, American should stay silent while a mad man is in power, with the power to change American, and move us back when white man ruled (period)!

But, because of all the crazy things Trump was saying and during, Obama could no longer stay quiet, he had to speak up and get back into the game.

With the election of the first black president, "Barack Obama" it cause an uprising among white people. White people (the Devil) started gathering their army. The war between good (God) and evil (the Devil) will be held in the sea of politics.

Before Moses had to use the power of God to force Pharaoh to let his people go, now God have to convince the people to let the Devil go.

The Devils army has now showed its hand (the Devil found his leader), Donald Trump. The war has now begun. The lines have now been drawn. Americans can no longer sit on the side line 'or' on the fence. It's time to act, register, and vote.

Now God is sending '3' powerful angels to lead the charge (the number '3' to let his people know it's him). One of his angel's was a man that was there with Martin L. King from the beginning, the other one nobody saw coming, and 3rd was a woman (a white woman). Now God is showing the Devil his hand (the battle is now on). "Choose ye this day", so says God.

If you don't get out and vote, a crazy man couldn't be back in the White House, someone with the power to change the human race 'or' end it. A dangerous person with his finger on the bottom that could end all man-kind. See, he is now trying to take away your health care.

Trump was now trying to over-turn all Obama legislation, mainly 'Obama care' his signature piece of legislation, he had to get back in the fight.

The Blue-Wave for Democratics took the country by storm. More women were elected to congress than any time in the history of America. A lot of women were also elected to state level government. The time for the future for women has come. God has now chose them to lead.

This is the first white person chosen by God, Nancy Patricia D' Alesandro Pelosi is an American politician serving as the Minority Leader of the United States House of Representatives since 2011, representing California's 12th congressional district. She previously served as the 52nd Speaker of the House from 2007 to 2011, the only woman to do so. Her ascent to House Speaker also made her the highest-ranking female politician in the history of the United States

The Blue-wave has been a movement with unprecedented potential in recent history. By many names, the prospect of a movement that proposes to restore the principles held by most Americans has been building, even if the Devil's in the White House.

Donald Trump will pay for what he's done, so will all the people that lie for him, and his family also. Since they wanted to play royal subjects to the king (they maybe indicted before the king). "You reap what you sow", so says God.

It is January 16, 2019 the Democracy Party can start making the Devil answer for his actions. Now that they have evidence form Mueller, the Democrat can finally do something.

So, even if nothing will be really done while Trump is still president (he could still be indicted when it's over). So, the next term is a must for Trump and a must for Democratic s to make sure it don't happen.

"Choose you this day whom ye shall serve...", so says God.

What house do you want to live in? God's House, then change your party from the Devil's party to God's party, the Democracy Party,

Remember Satan will gather his army from one shore (Russia) to one shore (Unity State of America) then battle for all mankind will be held in the sea of politics. The Devil can't win, 'so' please! Please!! Register, and vote.

This is where God re-eveleted woman, man had become only for himself. Then God showed man he was right 'by' sending the most powerful woman in congress to confront the Devil in his own house (the White House).

While this weak man sat, with his legs spread, waving his small hands, and sounding un-presidential (talking about a WALL) something that will never be built. This powerful lady, head of the party that just took the House in a land slide, explain to him what that meant. He probably still didn't get it, since he has the IQ of a 2 year old.

Year of the woman? Yes.

How that you're seen what happens in the Devil's House (tax bills for the rich) greed and money the materials that pads the road to HELL 'or' God's House where there's heath care for all Americans, more jobs, and you may save your soul from the Devil (which house do you choose)?

There are only 2 hands to play (power, politics, money) this is the hand the Devil plays 'or' (forgiveness, becoming saved, everlasting life) this is the hand God offers. "Choose you this day whom ye shall serve..." So says God.

Now that the field for president is large, remember cream rises to the top, when the best person has won (support her/him). Don't make the mistake of the past. Put all your support behind the winner, make all your supports back the winner, and defeat the Devil (Donald Trump). "The world can no longer survive Trump" so says God.

Everyone has been waiting for over a year for Mueller's report trying to guest what it might say. It is Friday March 22, 2019, Mueller submitted his report to the DOJ. Now everyone is waiting to see all the wrongs the president has committed, how bad, and if they reach the level of impeachment.

But no matter what the report may say, the people with Trump will still be with Trump, the people that think he should be impeached will still think that, and nothing will have really changed (only the election will do that).

So, no matter what the report says, all Democratic need to come together, get out the vote, and vote him out. Let's all Democratic stand-up and say, "we are better than this", then let's vote the Devil (Donald Trump) out by a landslide

To all Democratic, now that the Mueller report is out, people can see for themselves, and make their own judgements. Even if the AG (Barr) tried to paint a different picture. A picture that made Donald Trump look like someone that was the victim. The report sample shows how bigger liar, dishonest, and cheater he really is. Something everybody already knew, before he was elected president (with the help from the Russians).

The reason Donald Trump love dictators, they are all disciples of Satan. Dictation is done by fear. All dictators control this way. Fear is one of the Devil's beat tools. This is now Trump wants to govern and if we as Americans don't stop him (he will).

So, if you rush to impeach him, the people that stand with him will still be with him, those are the demons of Satan, they will always follow the Devil (Donald Trump). Sometimes we have to bite the bullet (so to speak), for the good of the country. But you should investigate everything, allowing the country to see everything, then people can judge for themselves, and let the poles decide 'or' impeach if the evidence say's that (don't be afraid to impeach). Because Democratics follow the law no matter where it takes them.

Remember something, just like God has his angels, Satan has his devils all over the world serving him. Satan has his armies all over the world with his devils (dictators) leading them. His armies are the demons from the angels that were rejected by God after the flood. Now they are the armies waiting for their leader. Satan found his leader in America (Donald Trump), that's why the people that follow him will always follow him (they are the servants of the devil). Only Satan can change their minds. "Choose ye this day whom you shall serve" so says God.

Now do what you need to do, send out a rattling call to all God's people, get them all registered, get them all to the poles, and make sure they all vote. "Evil will not win", so says God.

The End.

Last response from God

GOD ALLOW HIS ONLY son to die for the sins of man (Jesus). He die on the cross for the sins of man 'so' that man could live the life he wanted. God gave his only son (Jesus) 'so' man could be free to live "thank of that" all man have to do is live a righteous life (that's it).

Jesus begged his father on the cross to save him from death (although he knew he was already saved) in heaven. See, no man wants to die (not even Jesus) because when you die you leave all your family, and friends behind. You know, you will never see them again 'but' if you believe in God (you will) see them again (in heaven).

Jesus felt the same way as man (even though he was saved in heaven), he still didn't want to leaves his family, and friends behind. Jesus knew that after his death, he would return to the chosen one's in sprit from (not human form) before God descends him into heaven.

God allowed his only son Jesus to die, for the sake of man. What man living today would do that (for anything) God did it for the sake of man. The sins of man can simply be forgiven 'by' asking his son Jesus Christ for forgiveness, because he died for the sins of the whole human race.

Then, God allow his son to return home to live with the father 'so' when your sons return home (don't cast them out) because 'if' it's excepted by God then it should surely be excepted by all his people.

When you ask God to save you through his son Jesus Christ you will be forgiven, and saved. God knows your inter-most thoughts (those secrets you though only you knew), 'surprise' he knows. So, think Godly thoughts (he will know if you don't).

Only the pure in heart shall see God, he knows if your heart is pure or not. You can fool yourself, everyone else, 'but' you can't fool God (to thy own self be true). Now that the Devil have shown his hand, it's time to see if your heart is pure or not.

"When you have reap what you soy (seem the error of your ways) you will end up in HELL or HEAVEN", God's final words to the whole human race

"When you truly know God (only the pure in-heart) it takes you to another place, a place of higher understanding", and that's my final words.

Printed in the United States
By Bookmasters